CONTEST WINNERS FOR THREE

Piano Trios from the Alfred, Belwin, and Myklas Libraries

Foreword

Three is not always a crowd when making beautiful music at the piano! *Contest Winners for Three* is a time-tested collection of imaginative trios that can be an exciting part of any piano studio's curriculum, continuing to bring smiles to performers and audiences for years to come.

Alfred, Belwin, and Myklas have produced an extensive list of quality elementary- and intermediate-level piano trios over the years. The pieces included in this volume represent well-loved and effective trios drawn from festival and contest lists, presented in approximate order of difficulty. Divided into five graded collections, outstanding pieces are made available again by Jonathan Aaber, Dennis Alexander, Mary Elizabeth Clark, Margaret Goldston, Joyce Grill, Carrie Kraft, Sharon Lohse Kunitz, Beatrice Miller, Ruth Perdew, and Robert D. Vandall.

Contents

Alfred Music
P.O. Box 10003
Van Nuys, CA 91410-0003
alfred.com

ISBN-10: 0-7390-9929-9
ISBN-13: 978-0-7390-9929-2

Hot Pursuit

Part 3

Robert D. Vandall

Vivace

RH as written

mf   *mp*

LH 1 octave lower than written throughout

5

10

Part 2   **Vivace**

Both hands as written

mf   *p*

5

Hot Pursuit

Part 1

Robert D. Vandall

Part 2

4

Part 3

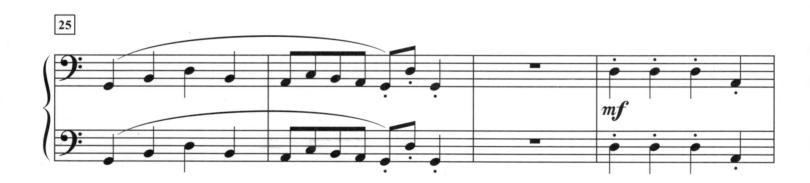

Part 2

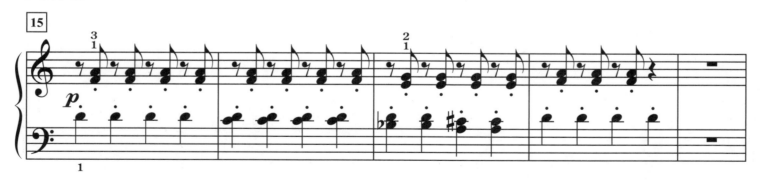

Part 1

Part 2

Part 3

Part 2

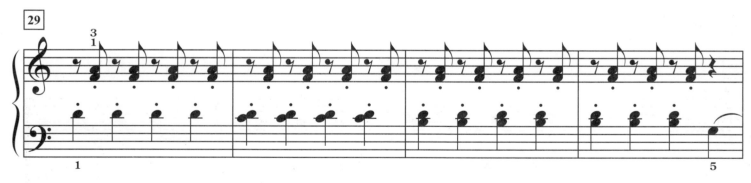

Part 1

Part 2

Down by the Riverside

Part 3

African-American spiritual
Arr. Beatrice A. Miller

Down by the Riverside

Down by the Riverside

Part 1

African-American Spiritua
Arr. Beatrice A. Mille

Down by the Riverside

African-American spiritual
Arr. Beatrice A. Miller

Part 3

Down by the Riverside

Part 1

African-American Spiritual
Arr. Beatrice A. Miller

Part 2

Part 3

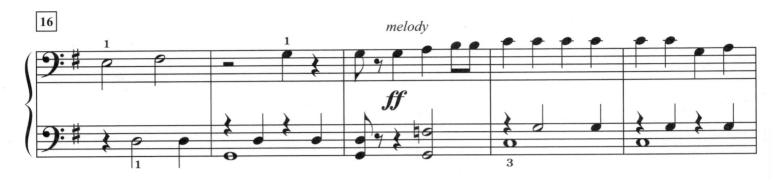

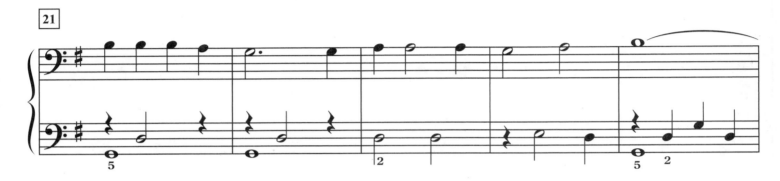

Part 2

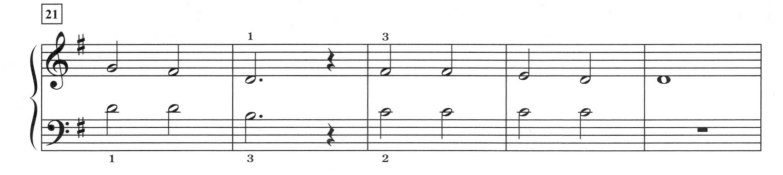

Part 1

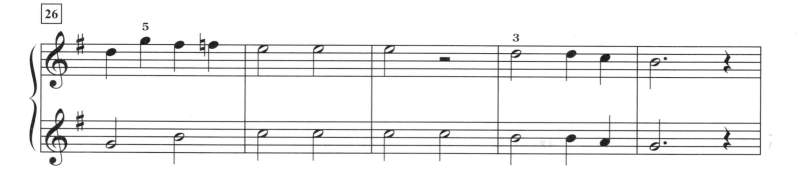

Part 2

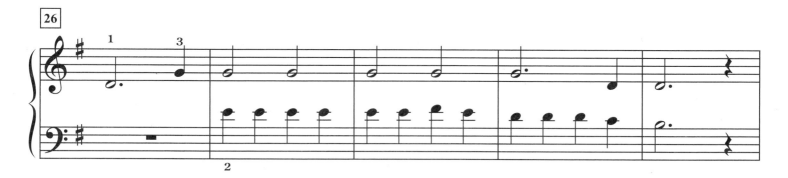

Part 3

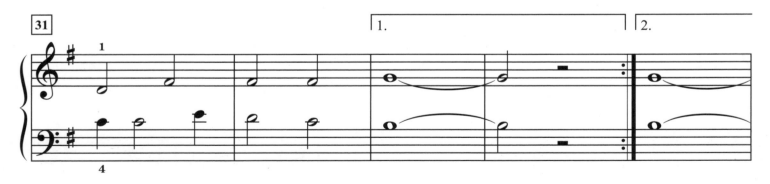

Part 2

Part 1

Part 2

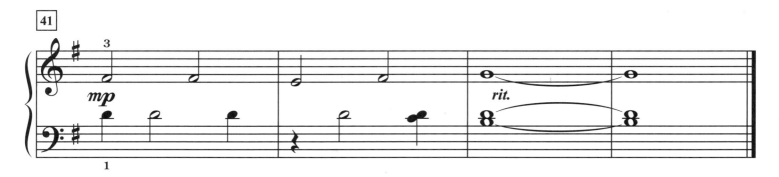

Three's a Crowd Rag

Part 3

Joyce Grill

Part 2

Three's a Crowd Rag

Part 1

Joyce Grill

Part 2

Part 3

Part 2

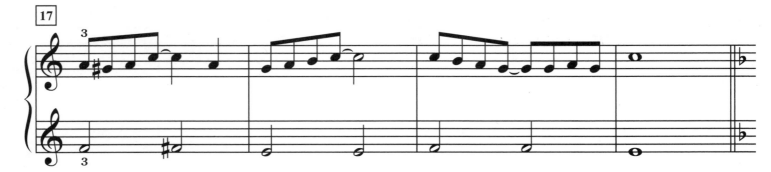

Part 1

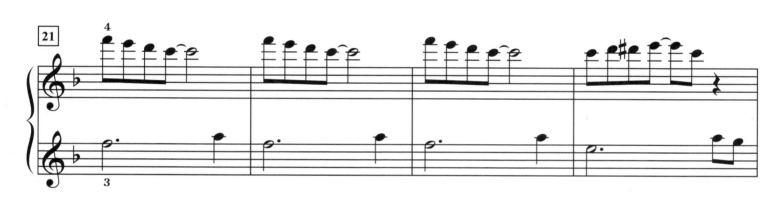

Part 2

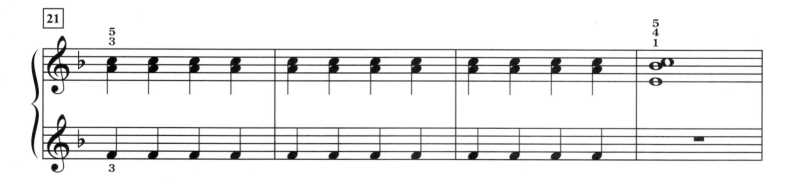

Part 3

Part 2

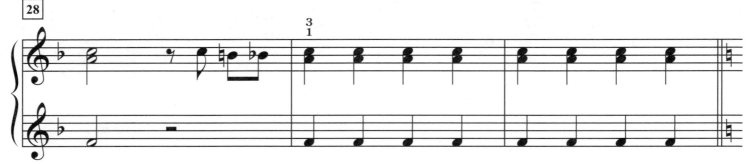

Part 1

Part 2

Part 3

Part 2

Part 1

(Player one gets pushed off the bench.)

(Player one stands behind players two and three, between the two players.)

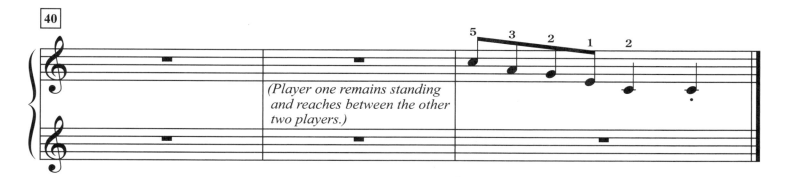

(Player one remains standing and reaches between the other two players.)

Part 2

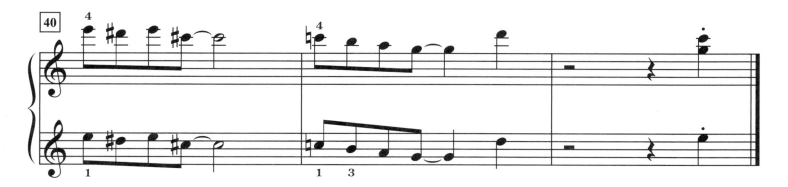

Cancún Cha-Cha-Cha

Part 3

Joyce Grill

Part 2

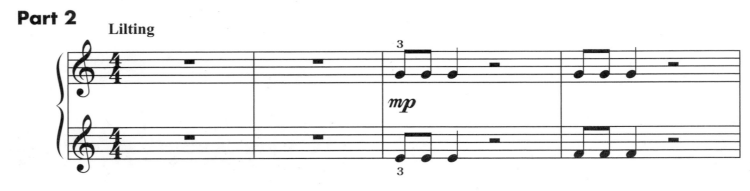

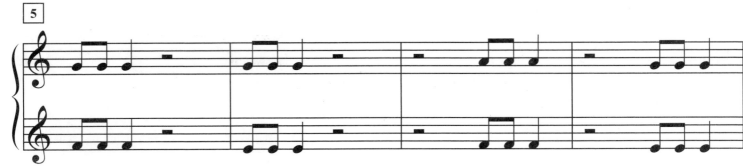

Cancún Cha-Cha-Cha

Part 1

Joyce Grill

Part 2

Part 3

Part 2

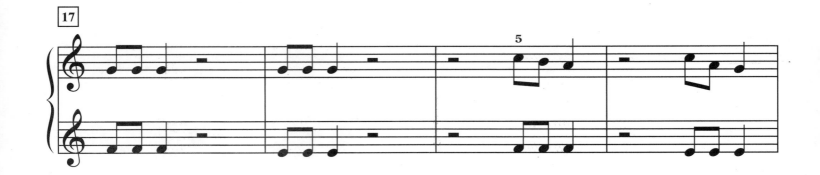

Part 1

Part 2

Yankee Doodle

Traditional
Arr. Beatrice A. Miller

Part 3

Lively

Both hands 1 octave lower than written

Part 2

Lively

RH as written

LH 1 octave higher than written throughout

Yankee Doodle

Part 1

Traditional
Arr. Beatrice A. Miller

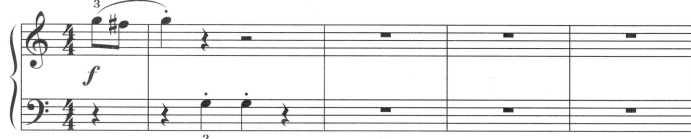

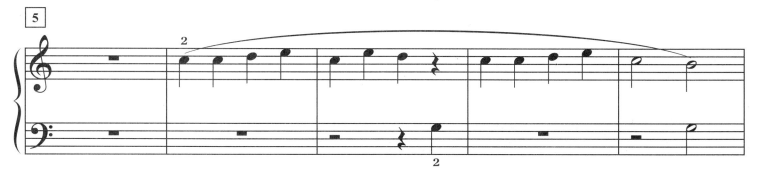

Part 2

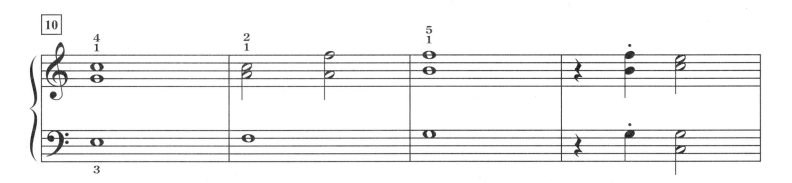

Part 3

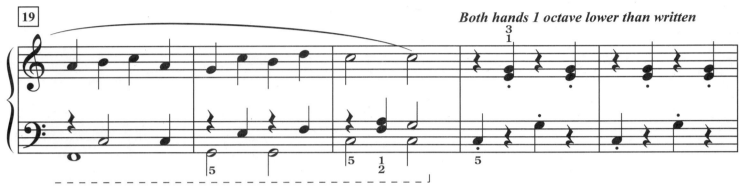

Part 2

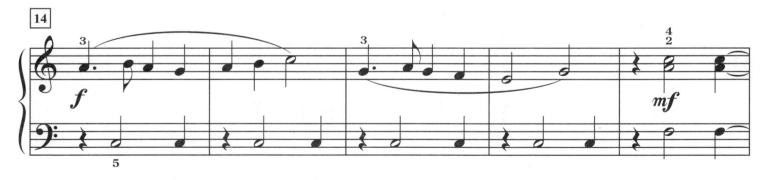

Part 1

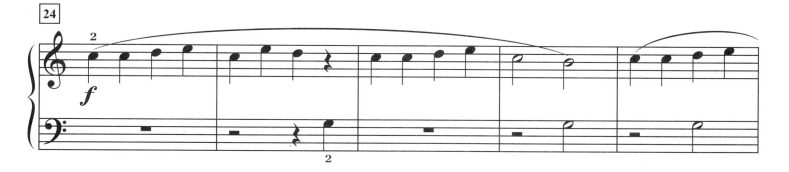

Part 2

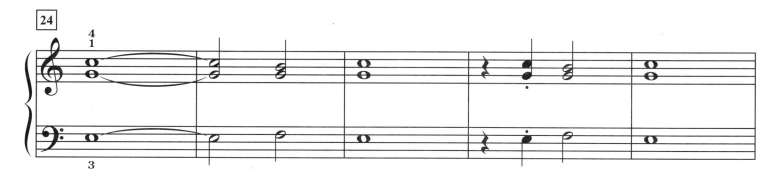

30

Part 3

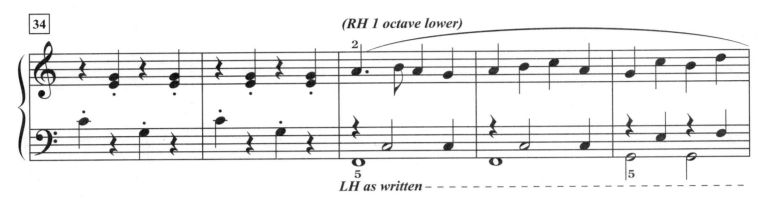

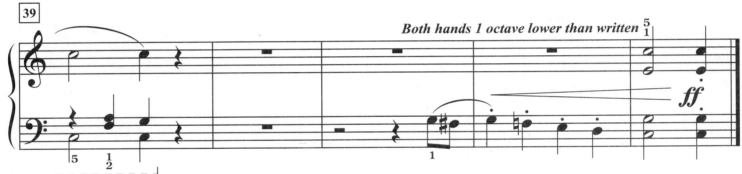

Part 2

Part 1

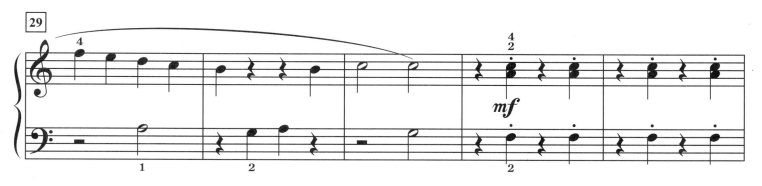

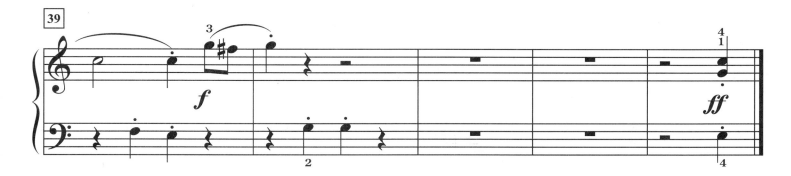

Part 2

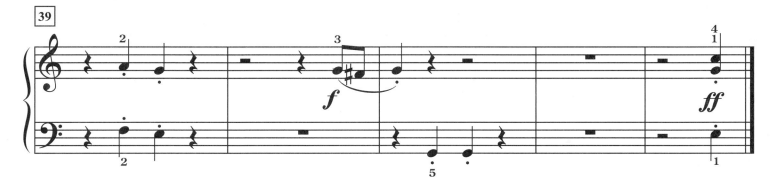

Alfred